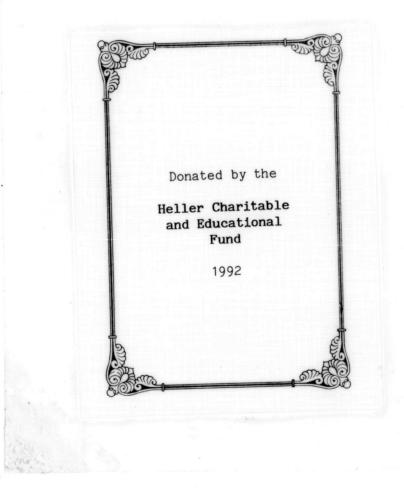

LA HISTORIA DE NAVIDAD

según los Evangelios de Mateo y Lucas

LA HISTORIA DE NAVIDAD

con ilustraciones de Jane Ray

DUTTON CHILDREN'S BOOKS   NUEVA YORK

Para Ellen

92-B1563

*Las palabras de los Evangelios según Mateo y Lucas han sido
tomados de la Santa Biblia, Ediciones Paulinas 1974.*

15.95

Derechos de ilustraciones © 1991 Jane Ray

CIP Data is available.

Reservados todos los derechos.

Publicado por primera vez en los Estados Unidos por
Dutton Children's Books
una división de Penguin Books USA Inc.

Originalmente publicado en 1991 en Gran Bretaña
por Orchard Books, the Watts Group,
96 Leonard Street, London EC2A 4RH

Primera edición Americana   Impreso en Singapur
10 9 8 7 6 5 4 3 2 1
Edición en inglés disponible
ISBN 0-525-44830-6

En tiempos de Herodes, Rey de Judea, había una joven
virgen que era prometida de José. Vivía en la ciudad de
Nazaret, y se llamaba María.

Entró el ángel Gabriel y le dijo: «Alégrate tú, la Amada
y Favorecida; el Señor está contigo. No temas, María,
darás a luz a un hijo, al que pondrás el nombre de Jesús.
Será grande entre los hombres y con razón lo llamarán

con María, su esposa, que estaba encinta.

Cuando estaban en la ciudad de David,

Hijo del Altísimo, y su reino no terminará jamás.»
Dijo María: «Yo soy la esclava del Señor; que se haga
en mí lo que has dicho.» Después de estas palabras
el ángel se retiró.

En esos días, el emperador, Cesar Augusto,
dictó una ley que ordenaba hacer un censo

en todo el imperio. Todos iban a inscribirse
a sus respectivas ciudades.

También José subió a Judea, para inscribirse

llamada Belén, le llegó el día que debía
tener su hijo.

Y dio a luz a su primogénito, lo envolvió en
pañales y lo acostó en un pesebre, porque no
había lugar para ellos en la posada.

En la región había pastores que vivían en el campo y que por
la noche se turnaban para cuidar sus rebaños. El ángel del
Señor se les apareció, y rodeó de claridad la gloria del Señor, y
todo esto les produjo un miedo enorme. Pero el ángel les dijo:
«No teman, porque yo vengo a anunciarles una buena nueva

que será motivo de mucha alegría para todo el pueblo. Hoy
nació para ustedes en la ciudad de David un Salvador que es
Cristo Señor. En esto lo reconocerán: hallarán a un niño
recién nacido, envuelto en pañales y acostado en un pesebre.»

De pronto aparecieron otros ángeles y todos
alababan a Dios, diciendo: «Gloria a Dios

en lo más alto del cielo, y en la tierra gracia
y paz a los hombres.»

Después que los ángeles volvieron al cielo, los
pastores comenzaron a decirse unos a otros:
«Vamos, pues, hasta Belén y veamos lo que ha

sucedido y que el Señor nos dio a conocer.»
Fueron apresuradamente y hallaron a María, a
José y al recién nacido acostado en un pesebre.

Entonces contaron lo que los ángeles
les habían dicho de este niño, y todos

Encaminándolos a Belén les dijo: «Vayan y averigüen bien
lo que se refiere a este niño. Cuando lo hayan encontrado
avísenme para ir yo también a adorarlo.»

En cuanto el rey les dijo esto, partieron.
La estrella que habían visto en Oriente iba

se maravillaron de lo que decían los pastores.

Habiendo nacido Jesús en Belén de Judá, durante el reinado de Herodes, vinieron unos Magos de Oriente a Jerusalén,

preguntando: «¿Dónde está el rey de los judíos que ha nacido?, porque hemos visto su estrella en el oriente y venimos a adorarlo.»

Herodes quedó preocupado al oírlos y también todos en
Jerusalén. Herodes entonces llamó privadamente a los Magos
para que le informaran cuándo se les había aparecido la estrella.

delante de ellos, hasta que se paró sobre
el lugar en que estaba el niño.

Hallaron al niño con María, su madre. Se postraron para
adorarlo y sacaron de sus cofres regalos y le ofrecieron oro,
incienso y mirra. Luego regresaron a su país por otro camino,
porque se les avisó en sueños que no volvieran donde Herodes.

Y el Ángel del Señor se le apareció en sueños a José y le dijo:
«Levántate, toma al niño y a su madre, y huye a Egipto, porque
Herodes buscará al niño para matarlo.» José se levantó, tomó
al niño y a su madre y se retiró a Egipto.

Después de la muerte de Herodes, José tomó al niño y a su madre, y se vino a Nazaret. Y el niño crecía, y se hacía cada día más sabio. Y la gracia de Dios estaba en él.

THE INCREDIBLE WORLD OF PLANTS

THE VEGETATION OF RIVERS, LAKES, AND SWAMPS

CHELSEA HOUSE PUBLISHERS
New York • Philadelphia

Text: Andreu Llamas
Illustrations: Luis Rizo

La vegetacion en los rios, lagos y pantanos © Copyright
EDICIONES ESTE, S. A., 1995, Barcelona, Spain.

The Vegetation of Rivers, Lakes, and Swamps copyright ©
1996 by Chelsea House Publishers, a division of Main Line
Book Co. All rights reserved.

1 3 5 7 9 8 6 4 2

Library of Congress Cataloging-in-Publication Data

Llamas, Andreu.
    [Vegetación en los ríos, lagos y plantanos. English]
    The vegetation of rivers, lakes, and swamps / [text, Andreu
Llamas ; illustrations, Luis Rizo].
        p. cm. — (The Incredible world of plants)
    Includes index.
    Summary: Describes the various plants that live in rivers,
lakes, swamps, and other bodies of water and explains how
they support other forms of life.
    ISBN 0-7910-3469-0. — ISBN 0-7910-3488-7 (pbk.)
    1. Aquatic ecology—Juvenile literature. 2. Aquatic plants—
Juvenile literature. [1. Aquatic plants. 2. Aquatic ecology.
3. Ecology.] I. Rizo, Luis, ill. II. Title. III. Series: Llamas, Andreu.
Incredible world of plants.
QH541.5.W3L5813   1996   95-22431
574.5′2632—dc20   CIP
                                                        AC

CONTENTS

PONDS AND LAGOONS

Water areas such as rivers, lakes, and ponds are some of the richest in animal and vegetable life. This is because there is water, food, and shelter for many different life forms.

Water areas form when rainwater comes down the mountains and, little by little, gathers in small currents and streams. Sometimes, however, the water is trapped and cannot continue to flow. This is when ponds are formed.

There are many more organisms in small ponds and streams than appear at first sight. In each area of a pond there are different species of plants and animals; for instance, the surface or just below the surface is the favorite place of many small swimmers and skaters that breathe air.

The animals and plants that live in still water are very different from those in fast waters as many factors change: water temperature, amount of oxygen, the form and composition of the *bed*.

In lagoons, the bed is muddy and plants decompose easily in the still waters. Few plants can grow in the fast stream currents, but in lakes and ponds the abundance of vegetation helps many animals to live.

Nevertheless, water environments are not always safe: lagoons, ponds, and even large lakes can freeze during the winter, killing many animals.

(1) Plant distribution
Plants are distributed according to their preferences either on shore or in the water.

(2) Water lentils
Each of the leaves you see on the surface is really a plant. New leaves are formed from old ones and fall off to form new plants. From each old leaf two new ones may grow.

(3) Algae
Microscopic algae, which serve as food to many small animals can be found covering the rocks on the bed.

(4) Air to breathe
Many small animals live in ponds but still need air to breathe. They have developed different strategies to do this. The rat's tail's larva (4a) has tube to breathe from the surface while remaining underwater. Water beetles (4b) always carry a storage of air with them that they frequently renew on the surface; they are like divers. Freshwater snails (4c) also come up to the surface, where they stay until they have renewed their stocks of air.

2

4c

4b

4a

5

POND PLANTS

To live in ponds, plants have had to develop special features that are different from those of land plants.

All ponds have many different types of vegetation that are distributed according to their preferences: on the edge of the water, near the shore, on damp land. In the intermediate zone, the plants always have their roots in the water, and there are the totally aquatic plants which live in the pond itself. The most common plants in ponds are rushes and sedges. Rushes have no leaves and their stalks are long and round. By contrast, sedges have stalks with a triangular section and their leaves are hard and pointed and come out of the stalk in three directions. Some of the most interesting plants in areas of still water such as ponds and lagoons are the floating plants that stay on the surface, such as water lentils. Water plantains and water lilies have their roots buried in the mud on the bed but their stalks are long so their leaves and flowers manage to appear on the surface. Their stalks also have air channels for the oxygen to go down from their leaves to their roots.

Ponds do not stay the same year after year. Normally, mud and dead plants accumulate on the bottom, and as the ponds become shallower, the rushes on the shore go closer to the middle. If this process continues, ponds can gradually become marshes, and eventually, forests.

Yellow lily
It has sword-shaped leaves, its flowers are yellow, and when they fade they form fruit capsules like thick pea pods that hold several seeds.

A

B

C

D

The incredible metamorphosis of frogs
A. The frog spawn is a mass of eggs surrounded by protective gelatin. B. After two weeks legless tadpoles with gills emerge. C. The rear legs appear after five to eight weeks, but they still swim with their tails. The gills have disappeared and they have to go up to the surface to breathe with their lungs. D. After three months they have four legs and a tail. E. When the tail has disappeared, it can still take up to 3 years to become adults.

E

Water plantain
They grow in the mud on the banks of streams and small rivers.

Rushes and sedges
They are the most common plants in ponds. They have hard stalks which last all winter and are used in many ways.

7

Water lilies

Water lilies are aquatic plants with leaves that float on the surface of still lake waters and in the middle and lower *reaches* of rivers.

Their leaves are very special: they are rounded, so they are protected when the wind blows on the surface of the pond and do not tear; and the leaves are covered in a waxlike substance that makes water slip on the surface of the leaves and prevents them from getting soaked.

Each floating leaf has small orifices or pores called stomas that are on the top of the leaf so that it can breathe. Land plants have these stomas under their leaves. These pores enable the exchange of gases necessary for breathing and food making. Part of the food produced by water lilies during *photosynthesis* is kept in a thick underwater stalk called a *rhizome*, which is anchored to the mud on the pond bed. While many water lilies die during the winter, the rhizomes survive and grow new stalks in spring.

To stay upright and floating, water lilies have air chambers that contain oxygen. The flowers also need to get onto the surface so that insects can pollinate them. Water lily flowers know how to guard themselves in adverse conditions; if it rains or is too cold, they close to protect the pollen inside. The leaves and the flowers float on the water, but when night falls the flowers close and sometimes even go underwater until the following morning.

Fierce hunters
These water beetles are ferocious hunters and do not hesitate to attack prey larger than themselves, such as fish or frogs.

Giants
In some parts of the Amazon River there are giant water lilies of over 7 feet (2 meters) in diameter! They float thanks to their thousands of air pockets, and you can see insects, birds, and lizards on them.

Floating fruit
Water lily flowers become egglike fruit after flowering. Their stalks bend so the fruit can grow underwater. At the right moment, the fruit (full of seeds) falls off the mother plants and floats away.

Snail eggs
When spring comes, each adult snail lays some 400 eggs under leaves. The eggs are stuck to the lower surface of the water lily leaf by means of a gelatin cord that also protects them and gives them food.

Stems
Water lily stems are strong but flexible so they can keep the flowers on the surface of the water but also withstand the water's movement.

STREAMS

In streams and torrents, the water runs fast and hard so their inhabitants must be able to withstand the current.

Water has a great capacity to *erode* and excavate the bed, so the banks tend to be quite steep. The water is cold and holds a lot of oxygen, but there are not many plants and animals able to stay there and use it. The plants that manage to stay hold on to the bottom or on to rocks with strong roots. Many of these plants have long stalks, and some even have split leaves to reduce their resistance to the water. However, other plants prefer to have two kinds of leaves: some are wide and float on the surface, while others are much finer and stay underwater (one example of this is the water spike).

There are also some plants that usually live in lakes and lagoons but have also adapted to life in rivers and streams. Animals have also developed systems to beat the current: some are very strong swimmers, like fish and freshwater crustacea, and others, such as leeches, prefer to hang on to rocks. Carp and eels swim among the plants while leeches and snails drag themselves over the stones.

If you watch a stream patiently, you will see many fish near the bottom looking for insect larvae and snails.

(1) Fighting the current
In mountain streams, the water passes hard between the rocks and stones. In these conditions, practically no vegetation can live.

(2) Toads
Unlike frogs, toads make a gelatinous necklace up to 7 feet (2 meters) long, which they roll around aquatic plants. The eggs are inside.

(3) Trout
Trout need to live in shallow currents of clear, cold waters that are rich in oxygen. They also need a stony bed to lay their eggs. (3a) 1st week: the interior of the egg is almost completely yolk. (3b) 5th week: the fry leave the egg but still carry the vitelline sack to feed on. (3c) Fry after 1 year.

(4) Leeches
To avoid being carried away by the current, leeches stick hard to rocks with suckers on their head and tail.

(5) Algae and moss
On the rocks on the floor of the stream, many different types of algae and moss may be seen, which make a green, slippery carpet. They are the only plants able to withstand the strong current.

5

2

3c

3b

1

3a

4

11

UNDERWATER PLANTS

On the floor of rivers and lakes there are some plants with long stalks. They compose underwater scenery that looks like strange forests where many small animals swim.

Some of these plants are so well adapted to life underwater that even their flowers open below the surface. Plants are essential for the survival of river animals: not only do they produce oxygen for the animals to breathe but they also provide them with shade and protect them from enemies such as the gray heron. These plants are the food of many different animals from insects to birds, and some also use them as a support to lay their eggs. Although the plants live underwater, they need to be well lit in order to receive the energy from the sun's rays to carry out photosynthesis. This is why they do not favor turbulent water. If you see a river with a lot of *sediment* and particles in suspension, there are likely to be very few plants underwater because they would not get enough light.

Generally, deep water plants tend to be rather delicate. This is because, as they are sustained by water, they do not need to form thick stalks. Out of the water, these plants are unable to stand up by themselves. On the other hand, underwater plants usually have small, thin leaves, because unlike land plants, they do not need to store water.

The volvox
This is what a volvox looks like. It is a microscopic water plant that is food to many lagoon inhabitants.

Living submerged
Ceratophylla are plants that are well adapted to living underwater. Their feather leaves spread under the surface and their flowers even open there.

12

A

B

C

D

Incredible insects
A. Adults lay eggs in gelatin on stones, both in and out of the water. B. When it leaves the egg, the larva makes a long, thin case where it hides. It takes grains of sand, leaves, twigs, and small shells and sticks them to the silk it secretes from its mouth. C. The larva spends almost a year feeding on the plants on the bed, then it closes the two ends of its protective tube and becomes a chrysalis. *D. Two weeks later, the case opens and the adult emerges and flies away.*

Hideout for fish
The stalks of some aquatic grasses are used as shelters and hideouts by many fish.

UNDERWATER PLANT REPRODUCTION

Aquatic plants have developed different ways to reproduce. Some of these techniques are very different from those used by plants that live on dry land.

Many are born from seeds that form after pollination, which can occur with the aid of the wind, with help from insects, and even in the water. When spring comes, many water plants cover themselves in flowers of striking colors and from each of their fruits more than 1,000 seeds may be freed.

There are other aquatic plants that reproduce by means of their underground stalks, or rhizomes. This system can have great advantages when bad weather approaches.

Some plants prefer not to reproduce by means of seeds, in which case new plants emerge from winter shoots or from fragments of stalk that have broken off the old plants.

The flowers of some water plants are very special; for example, water lily flowers remain closed in the morning and only open fully around midday. Then they close again at dusk and slightly submerge. Obviously, if the weather is bad or it rains, they decide not to open at all. There is an explanation to this capricious behavior: as well as protecting the flower from the weather, it only allows the flowers to be open when the pollinating insects are active.

A

B

Pollination
Here are three different types of pollination for aquatic plants:
a. with the aid of insects
b. with the aid of the wind
c. in the water

C

Diving spiders

The water spider can stay underwater for a long time as it builds an air store. What it does is to weave a sheet between submerged plants and fill it with air from the surface (held between the hairs on its abdomen).

Stalks that break

Some plants have fragile stalks that break very easily. A new plant forms from each piece!

Water fleas

Water fleas drag themselves along the floor and feed on remains in decomposition.

Spreading

Aquatic plants use different methods to spread their seeds.
a. with the aid of the wind
b. carried in the water
c. pods that explode; they open violently and the seeds fall some distance from the mother plant

A

B

C

LAGOONS IN SPRING AND SUMMER

The amount and variety of plants in a lagoon depends on the amount of light. If a lagoon receives too much shade from the trees on the shore, it will have very few plants as a result.

When spring comes, water lentils and small algae are the first plants to grow—since they are small they need little food. As the days become warmer, the animals in the lagoon start to leave the shelters among the plants and on the muddy bed. Frogs, toads, fish, and insects surprisingly appear all around and the plants and animals seem to be in a hurry to grow. Young ones are born very soon.

It is interesting to see how life awakens in small lagoons first, as the water warms faster than in deeper ones. The warmer the water is the faster the young develop.

In summer, the plants in lagoons and on the shores become covered in flowers of all colors and fruit even begins to form in some.

As summer passes, the young grow larger but their number has been greatly reduced as most have fallen into the mouths of predators. For the survivors, the end of the summer is the time to grow and fatten to face the unfavorable season.

Tadpoles
When summer arrives, tadpoles devour the abundant water plants in lagoons. However, they have many enemies such as fish, newts, water beetles, and dragonfly nymphs.

Rush flowers
When summer comes, the pink rush flowers open on the top of the stalks, about 5 feet (1.5 meters) tall.

Hidden nests
The nests of the common warblers are woven between reed stalks, using the reed flower heads and other vegetable remains. The nest is very deep so that the wind does not blow the eggs out.

Willows
Willows are trees that prosper living near the banks of rivers and lakes. Here you can see how their flowers (catkins) are pollinated by the wind.

Aquatic cuckoopint
Here you can see the strange fruit of the aquatic cuckoopint. The specialized leaves that surround them begin to fade and turn yellow.

Impatient flowers
When the last snows have disappeared, buttercup flowers are some of the first flowers to open.

Food for moths
Willow leaves are food to the caterpillars of some moths, such as this Cerura harpia.

17

LAGOONS IN AUTUMN AND WINTER

The plants and animals detect the change when autumn approaches. The hours of light become shorter day by day and there is a gradual drop in temperature.

During the autumn lagoon inhabitants prepare for the cold winter ahead.

The flowers have already become fruit in which the seeds wait to be spread. Many animals ceaselessly devour mature fruit to make energy stores in their bodies and, without realizing, contribute to the spreading of seeds. In other cases, the seeds of plants are spread by the autumn winds. There are some species like bulrush that keep their fruit throughout the winter and do not release their seeds until the following spring.

Winter creates very difficult conditions for the animals. As the water temperature drops, small animals such as snails move more slowly and seek refuge in deeper waters. Cold-blooded animals such as amphibians cool their bodies as the water around them cools, so they manage to greatly reduce the energy they need and survive almost without eating until the good weather returns.

In winter, many lagoons freeze but some submerged plants still succeed in carrying out photosynthesis with the sunlight that passes through the ice cap. Leaves that have fallen to the bottom of the water form a layer that protects the plant shoots and small animals that have sought refuge there, insulating them against the cold.

(1) The coming of the cold
The appearance of the lagoon changes with the coming of autumn. Animals and plants prepare their distinct strategies for combating the cold weather.

(2) Fungi
Autumn is the best season for fungi to grow. They can grow on the floor, between stones, or on branches. Here you can see some brasidiometes fungi growing on a tree trunk.

(3a) The anodon and rodeo fish
Anodons are mollusks that stop growing almost completely during the winter. One of the most surprising things that happens to anodons is that they are chosen by rodeo fish to lay their eggs inside.

(3b) The rodeo female chooses a living anodon and, with a special tube, lays some eggs in the mollusk's gills. (3c) The rodeo young come out after two or three weeks. The mollusk also benefits, as the anodon larvae come out stuck to the gills of the fry and can travel far away.

(4) Hiding from bad weather
When autumn comes, the leaves become covered in special scabs that increase their weight and make them sink to the bottom in order to avoid the winter freezing.

4

SHORES

River banks, also known as shores, are transformed as the river changes on its way to the sea.

River shores are very special: first, the water available means that deciduous trees grow on the shores a long way from their usual climates; second, the soil composition is different because it is made up of materials deposited by the river; and third, the plants are distributed in strips according to their preferences, and the periodic floods that the shores suffer force the plants to adapt in a very special way.

In the higher reaches of the river the water runs fast between the rocks, but as the current becomes slower, the river widens its bed and the banks become gentler.

If a river is very wide the current becomes so slow that many plants can spread roots and grow at the very edge of the water. In this case, the plants have very powerful roots that can withstand the floodwater in the rainy season. After the swell, there are remains on the branches that indicate how high the water has reached, and sometimes the water may rise several feet.

Willows are the trees that live nearest the river, since their flexible stalks make them very resistant to the rise in the water level. These trees are very important because their roots hold the soil and help to retain the materials the current drags away.

The shores of lakes and ponds also have soft soil where many different kinds of plants grow. On river banks there are many animals that dig tunnels to build their nests. The best known of these are the kingfisher, the water rat, and the otter.

(1) Reeds
Reeds grow in groups in marshes and on the banks of rivers and streams. Their stalks are long and straight and can grow up to 10 feet.

(2) Female runner
The female runner lives in shallow water near the banks. If you look closely you will see that this plant has tiny flowers (no petals) that sprout from the base of the leaves, right next to the stem.

(3) The crested newt
They spend much of their life on the shores of marshes or lagoons but underwater they become good swimmers using their fishlike tail. They have a great appetite and eat many small animals like crustacea, worms, insects, and even other newts.

(4) The terrible dithyscus
The dithyscus is a very fast hunter which can dive at speeds of up to 20 inches (50 centimeters) per second. It moves by means of its rear legs, which move like oars. (4a) It attacks just about any animal it meets and does not hesitate to attack larger animals, even frogs. (4b) The adults lay their eggs in grooves in aquatic plant stalks and the larvae that emerge are also terrible hunters with large jaws.

(5) The river crab
Here you can see what a river crab looks like. Although it does not hunt fish, it sometimes eats fish it finds sick or dead but which have not yet begun to decompose.

5

BEAVER DAMS

There are few animals able to change their surroundings as much as beavers do.

Beavers live in shallow lakes, streams, and slow, calm rivers. To survive they need an environment that does not dry up completely in summer and where water does not freeze down to the bottom in winter. They are incredible architects and engineers, capable of transforming the scenery by building enormous, complicated dams which can reach over 6 feet (2 meters) in height and 328 feet (100 meters) in length.

These dams allow the beavers to maintain a water level high enough that predators do not enter their burrows. This is why beavers regularly extract the mud from the bottom to prevent the water from becoming shallower with the accumulation of sediments.

Beavers are untiring woodcutters. Every beaver colony needs some 200 or 300 trees of 1 inch to 1 foot (3 to 30 centimeters) in diameter each year; to cut down a tree, a beaver only needs 10 or 15 minutes and sometimes they cut down trees more than 3 feet (1 meter) wide.

Despite some destruction, beaver dams are beneficial to their environment as they avoid the erosion of the soil by the rains. These dams also prevent streams from drying up completely in summer, which helps other animals like elk, deer, amphibians, and water birds.

Beavers are vegetarians. They eat grass, roots, water lily rhizomes, rushes, willow and poplar branches, among other things.

(1) Tons of vegetables
Beaver activity harms surrounding vegetation, since beavers have to accumulate several tons of vegetable material to build and maintain their dams.

(2) Dragonflies: great hunters
Dragonflies are very strong fliers that fly over the surface of the water looking for prey. (2a) Adults only live one month, so they concentrate most of their effort on reproducing. During fertilization, the male dragonfly holds the female down. (2b) The larva that comes out of an egg must change its skin between 8 and 15 times before becoming an adult. (2c) When summer comes, the nymphs climb onto a branch and the adult insects come out of their bodies, remaining on the plant for a few seconds until the new body hardens, opening their wings and flying away.

(3) Untiring
Beavers continually take branches to the dam to repair leaks.

3

1

2a

2b

2c

23

THE RIVER SOURCE

Rivers are born at the highest reaches where the rain or spring water forms a more and more defined channel. Here streams are narrow and shallow but it is very noisy when the water opens its way between the rocks.

River water comes from rain, filtration, and snow and glaciers melting, and rivers change constantly along their course. When a river is born, it begins its journey as a fast, bubbling mountain stream, but when it reaches the sea, it has become a wide river of slow, tranquil waters. The riverbanks also change along the journey, and their inhabitants (plants and animals) are different in each stretch. Cane plantations, for example, can only grow in areas of slow water.

In the higher reaches of the river, the half-submerged rocks are covered with moss on top and below, but the fast current prevents any other plants from growing. Plants cannot grow on the bottom of the water, and we can only find water asters and floating buttercups, which fold their flexible stalks giving way to the force of the current while remaining well-anchored to the floor. There are even few mosses as the current drags pebbles away!

The current is so strong that only a few adult insects and larvae manage to get hold of pebbles covered in mildew. Nevertheless, sometimes there are deeper wells where trouts, which are able to swim against the strong current, live.

(1) Using any corner
Life always takes advantage of any opportunity. Here you can see a plant that lives on the land trapped between large pebbles in the middle of the current.

(2) Abundant lichen
The damp shade on banks is the ideal place for many different species of lichens.

(3) Coupling dances
Ephemera live only a few days as adults, so they spend the most time trying to mate and lay eggs in the water. If you should ever see one, do not mistake it for a mosquito, as it has three long tails.

(4) Ferns
Ferns have a special shape and abound along riverbanks, in wet areas and in the shade. Ferns

reproduce by means of spores that they store in their sporangia under their leaves.

(5) Withstanding the current
Some plants, such as this fountain moss, can withstand the force of the current by holding on to a fallen trunk in the water or a rock in the torrent.

(6) The aquatic blackbird
The aquatic blackbird prefers to live on the banks of the fast waters of mountain torrents. It scrambles to look for food, especially small crustacea, fish, and insects in baths, that only last five to eight seconds. However, it scrambles more than 1,000 times a day.

(7) Covered with moss
Moss grows on many of the stones and tree trunks near rivers.

7

THE MIDDLE AND LOWER REACHES

As the river advances on its way to the sea, it widens and the current becomes slower.

As the water slows, banks of gravel form on the shores where plants such as buttercups can grow. In the middle reach, conditions may be very favorable for plants both on the banks and in the water. For instance, green algae with filaments form in masses on the edge of the water or among rocks and branches, where they shelter insect larvae. Many animals come to the water to drink, and it is very easy to find traces of them in the mud.

In the lower reach, the river is fed by the water from many *tributaries*, which sometimes are as big as the river itself. This stretch of river is very much like a pond, as the current is very slow, so it accommodates pond vegetation and animals. Mud accumulates on the banks, and cane, rushes, and reeds grow in many areas. These all have powerful roots that they use to hold on tightly to the bed and even withstand the violent rises in the water level in the rainy season. Willows and alders grow next to the gentle banks.

At this point, the river transports many particles in suspension and sediment that make it difficult for light to enter the water, so algae cannot live there. However, in areas where the current is slower, plankton made up of microscopic algae live and dye the water a dark green color.

The stones and dead branches that are in the water and receive sunlight are covered in a gelatinous layer made up of microscopic algae—diatoms—which proliferate by the thousand.

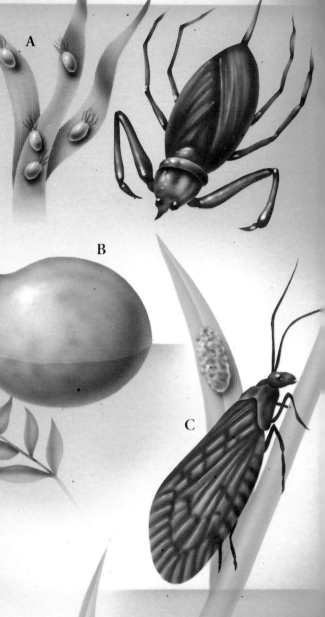

Choosing a place for the eggs
Insects choose the best place to lay their eggs. They always have the following possibilities: A. In the water, on underwater plants or stones, in the mud, or on the bed. B. On the surface of the water. C. Out of the water, on stalks and aquatic plants, leaves, and stones. D. In and out of the water. Some insects can lay their eggs both in and out of the water.

A   B   C

A nest below the water

A. When spring arrives, this male carp builds a hole in the sand with its stomach and fins, then it takes some aquatic plants and sticks them with mucous secreted from its kidneys. B. The vividly colored male attracts a female to its tunnel-shaped nest, where she lays from 100 to 400 eggs. C. The male looks after the eggs until they open and the young can look after themselves.

Vegetable plankton

In the lower reaches of rivers there are many nutrients, which allow the presence of numerous microscopic algae floating in the water.

A multicolored fisherman

Perching on a branch, the kingfisher spies passing fish and swoops down on its prey quickly.

MARSHY AREAS

Marshes are zones where the water and land are so mixed that they are often confused. They can receive many different names: salt marshes, swamps, or bogs.

Every marsh has its own characteristics. Some look like lakes while others are almost totally covered with cane plantations and look like meadows but are full of water during most of the year.

Marshy areas may have fresh- or saltwater. Saltwater marshes are on the coast near the estuary or river mouth as the saltwater comes from the sea.

On the other hand, freshwater marshes are often found near lakes or lagoons or also in areas where large rivers overflow and flood nearby areas every year. These marshy areas are usually on both sides of wide shallow rivers.

The water level in marshes can change with the seasons but the plants and animals have learned to adapt perfectly. The abundance of grass, cane, and rushes in these marshes give shelter to a great number of animals and birds, but also alligators and snakes.

(1) Water
In marshes, the water seems to have forgotten what direction it is going in.

(2) Walking on water
Some birds, such as this jacana, have very long fingers that enable them to walk on floating plants without sinking.

(3) Hunting in the water and on land
This ring snake likes to live in damp areas such as the shores of marshes, lagoons, and rivers. It is a hunter able to catch prey both in the water and on dry land. Its favorite diet is frogs, toads, tadpoles, small fish, and small birds.

(4) The life of the mosquito
(4a) A mosquito's life begins in water. Adults lay their eggs in the form of small rafts, on the surface of calm water. (4b) When they leave the eggs, the larvae float in the water, hanging head down. For three weeks they feed by filtering the food particles from the water. (4c) They become chrysalis and stay close to the surface so they can continue to breathe. (4d) When the time comes, the chrysalis opens and an adult emerges, which begins to fly as soon as it has unfolded its wings.

3

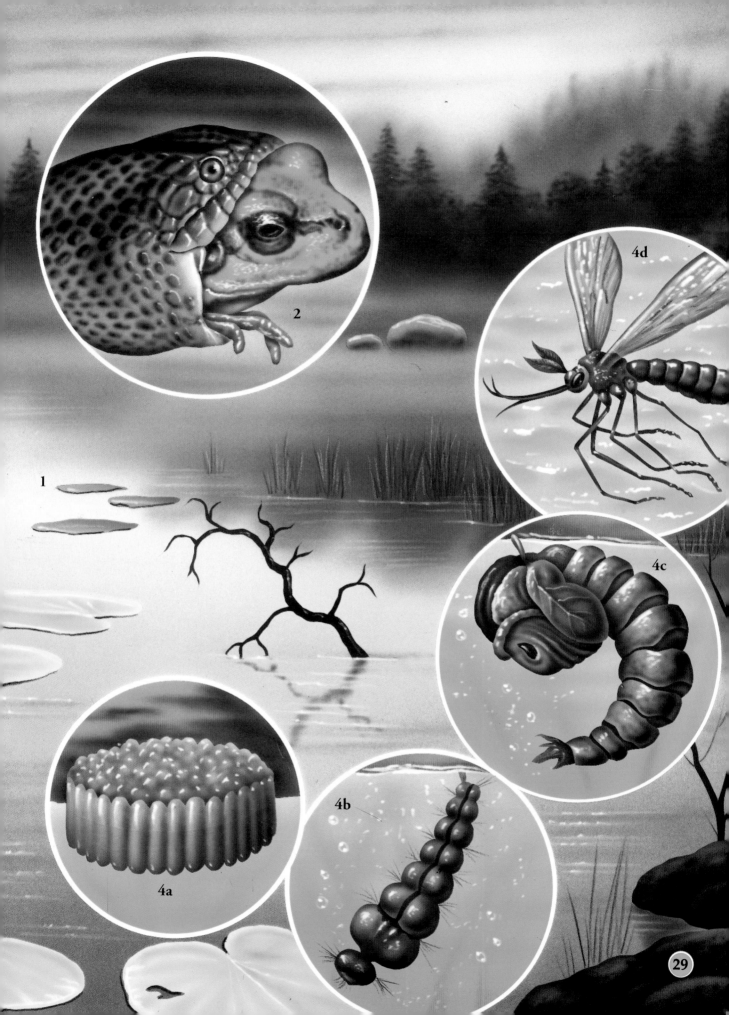

1

2

4a

4b

4c

4d

ESTUARIES AND DELTAS

An estuary is the lowest part of a river. This zone is so close to the sea that the effect of the tides is noticeable and there is a significant mix of fresh- and saltwater.

When the river runs into the sea it forms an estuary. On reaching the sea the two riverbanks separate until they become the seashore.

The area is greatly affected by tides: when the tide comes in, saltwater enters the river and the animals and plants notice its influence. But when the tide goes out, areas of mud may be uncovered that house a great deal of green, viscous algae, and it is also possible to see great extensions of salt marshes full of wild beet and spattered with saltwater wells.

As rivers approach the sea, their current virtually comes to a standstill so the particles the water was transporting fall to the bottom. The waves and tides also cloud the water; this is why few plants live submerged in estuaries as they can not get the light they need.

The accumulation of the sediments dragged along by the river or sea on the bed can give rise to very special environments, such as coastal lagoons or deltas. In deltas, the land dragged by rivers slowly gains land from the sea that stand out particularly for the spectacular number of birds that choose to live there.

By contrast, very few plants and animals have managed to adapt to the change in salt concentrations which are present in river mouths, so those that have done so have hardly any competition.

(1) Salt marshes
Here, rapid changes in salinity occur twice a day with the entry and exit of water from high and low tides. Very few living beings can withstand such conditions.

(2) Saltwort
These have fleshy leaves where they store water, and they are edible. They are well adapted to living in salt marshes and estuaries.

(3) Water fleas
The conditions created by the beaver dam help many animals such as water fleas, which are the food of larger predators.

(4) Floating islands
Here you can see how some pieces of dead seaweed, feathers, crab remains, and grass have come together to form a floating mass in the calm waters of the estuaries.

(5) Well-tested fish
Some fish, such as this flounder (flat fish) and the pipefish, have been able to adapt and can withstand the constant changes in salinity which occur in estuaries.

3

Glossary

bed the bottom of a body of water, especially an area supporting a heavy growth of a particular organism

chrysalis an insect that is in a protective covering while preparing for the last stage of its metamorphosis

erode to wear away by the continual action of water, wind, or glacial ice

photosynthesis a process in which green plants synthesize organic material through carbon dioxide, using sunlight as energy

reach a continuous stretch or expanse, especially a straight portion of a stream or river

rhizome a long, horizontal subterranean plant stem that is thickened by deposits of reserve food and produces shoots above and below the surface

sediment the matter deposited by wind or water that settles to the bottom of a liquid

tributary a stream feeding a larger stream or lake

Index

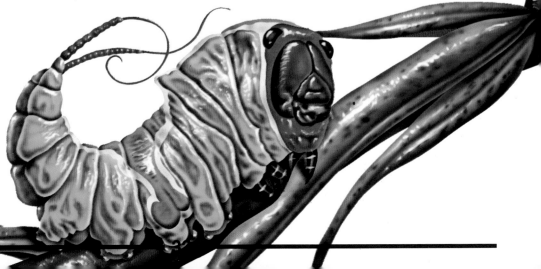